100 Tips for eBay
Buyers & Sellers

GLOBAL
PUBLISHING
G R O U P

Global Publishing Group
Australia • New Zealand • Singapore • America • London

GW00382299

What People Are Saying About 100 Magic Tips

Lee Moved His Traditional Business Online & Now Makes $30,000 A Month

"My name's Lee

I've been learning eBay from Matt & Amanda and it has really changed my life.

Over just about three years now I changed from my traditional business and now do over $30,000 in sales per month on eBay every month, at Christmas time over $50,000

I'm very happy about that and I can't thank them enough, thanks Matt & Amanda"

Lee, Brisbane

Kristian Made $1.4 M on eBay in 2010 & Is On Track To Make $3,000,000 In 2011

"I'd like to grab this opportunity to express my gratitude to Matt & Amanda.

I started with their course and found a product which has established a whole business for myself and my wife which has given us the lifestyle we always wanted.

It not just the eBay education, but also the business skills that has set us up for life. Also the mindset and everything we need for business and I really appreciate that.

We've basically built a business that last year turned over $ 1.4 Million and this financial year is set for $ 3,000,000 from one product that I found from going through Matt & Amanda's program so thanks very much for that."

Kristian, Gold Coast

100 Magic Tips for eBay

Buyers & Sellers

Discover
eBay's
Hidden
Secrets

Matt & Amanda Clarkson

World's Leading eBay Educators

FIRST EDITION 2011

Copyright© 2011 Matt & Amanda Clarkson

National Library of Australia
Cataloguing-in-Publication entry:

Clarkson, Matt, 1971-
100 magic tips for ebay buyers & sellers / Matt & Amanda Clarkson ; Darren Stephens.

1st ed.
ISBN: 9781921630460 (pbk.)

eBay (Firm)
Internet auctions.
Internet marketing.
Electronic commerce.
Success in business.

Other Authors/Contributors:
Clarkson, Amanda, 1965-
Stephens, Darren, 1964-

381.177

Published by Global Publishing Group
PO Box 517 Mt Evelyn, Victoria 3796 Australia
Email info@TheGlobalPublishingGroup.com

For Further information about orders:
Phone: +61 3 9736 1156 or Fax +61 3 8648 6871

From Matt and Amanda Clarkson…eBay Power Sellers, International Speakers and Best Selling Authors.

Whether you're just starting out on eBay, or perhaps a seasoned seller or buyer, this little eBay Magic hand book is sure to give you some great ideas on how you can grow your business faster, make more profits or buy smarter if that's what you love to do.

Here's a tiny insight into what other successful sellers and buyers are doing, which sees them enjoying all the benefits that buying and selling on eBay can give you once you know what you're doing.

We dedicate this book to anyone who dares to take charge of their destiny and isn't afraid to ask for help along the way.

Here's to you. Enjoy.

Matt & Amanda Clarkson

Acknowledgements

It has been an honour, a privilege, and a life goal achieved by writing this book. As with any major project or business success, there are many very special people who have contributed to our growth, making it possible for us to achieve our goals, and ultimately to making this book happen. So, we'd like to take this opportunity to say "THANK YOU".

Firstly, we'd like to thank our thousands of eBay Magic members who were the inspiration for this book.

Next, a huge thanks to our own wonderful in house dream team who support us while we work tirelessly to coordinate and pull all the material together for this book, as well as our ongoing efforts to spread the word on what's possible with an eBay business.

Thank you Genta Capan, Tamra Forde & Rachelle. You're an outstanding team and are the glue that holds this wild ride together!

We thank our friends and partners Darren & Jackie Stephens for their amazing talent, feedback and support.

A huge Thank You to our Awesome publisher Global Publishing Group for your dedication and commitment to the books.

Contents

FREE BONUS

To Claim Your
FREE Report, Your
DVD & Special
Audio MP3 Gift
With A Total Value
of **$297** visit...

www.biddingbuzz.com/book

50 Magic Tips for eBay Buyers

eBay is a fantastic way to shop from the comfort of your own home and these Magic Tips will help you score some amazing deals on eBay!

1

Once you register for a 'buyers account' on eBay you can watch up to 200 items in the 'My eBay' watching area, to keep track of any bargains you find.

2

You can also sort the items you're watching into specific lists, including a watch list, gift ideas, research and wish list or you can create your own list.

3

Because eBay uses a proxy bidder to bid on your behalf, it's not always best to put in the maximum amount you're willing to bid. Instead, wait until the last few minutes before bidding.

4

Proxy bidding is a program that bids on your behalf and, when you place a bid, you enter the maximum amount you're willing to pay for the item and eBay then bids against other buyers in increments starting at 50 cents. This means that the price can dramatically increase depending on what you and your competition have entered as a maximum price.

5

When you enter your maximum price, enter in an odd amount, for example $10.63, instead of a flat rate. This way you can outbid someone by a few cents instead of a large increment.

6

You can also use 'sniping' tools such as **www.hammersnipe.com** that will bid on your behalf in the last few seconds of an auction ending. The best bit is, you don't even have to be online!

7

Many people make a decent income from 'arbitraging' from eBay sellers who have no clue what they're doing wrong. To do this you should look for sellers with little to no feedback and sellers that have poor photos or even no photos at all! (You'll need to be familiar with the make or model if there's no pictures, so you can re-sell it).

8

When arbitraging, do a search in eBay for an item and then 'sort' the results to what you're specifically looking for. This could be 'the time ending soonest' or 'price and postage lowest first' to snipe cheap items.

9

Or how about searching for items that are 'distance nearest' first? A lot of sellers can't be bothered packing their items up and shipping them out so you can make a tonne of money from picking the item up locally (and saving on postage yourself) and then reselling it with worldwide shipping available.

10

If you've ever wondered why items with weeks to go appear before items with only hours to go in the search results, it's because the 'items ending soonest' don't automatically show up at the top any more. eBay's 'best match' search engine system sorts the results out based on what they feel the buyer would be looking for, and match it with the most professional sellers, based on their feedback and successful listing results.

"Your life can change in an instant…when you decide to leave the past behind as it has nothing to do with your future."

Amanda Clarkson

"It's in a moment of decision your destiny is created."

Darren J Stephens

11

Or how about searching for items that are 'distance nearest' first? A lot of sellers can't be bothered packing their items up and shipping them out so you can make a tonne of money from picking the item up locally (and saving on postage yourself) and then reselling it with worldwide shipping available.

12

If you've ever wondered why items with weeks to go appear before items with only hours to go in the search results, it's because the 'items ending soonest' don't automatically show up at the top any more. eBay's 'best match' search engine system sorts the results out based on what they feel the buyer would be looking for, and match it with the most professional sellers, based on their feedback and successful listing results.

13

While you're there, why not have a look at what else that seller has listed for sale? Quite often you can combine the postage from two or more items purchased from the one seller, which means your end price will be lower per item.

14

When searching for items on eBay, they make it easier to 'niche' down to what you're specifically looking for with the 'Item Specifics' in the left hand column. You can niche down into categories, condition, price, listing formats, location and more, to save you time.

15

Often sellers will list items in the incorrect category or with no item specifics. So, don't limit yourself to shopping in the categories that are obvious to you or for items that only have the specifics filled out; many a bargain can be found hiding if you look closely!

16

You can also save searches if you're looking for a particular item that may not be listed at that exact time. This means eBay will notify you via email for up to 12 months if that item gets listed.

17

The saved searches are also a valuable tool if you plan on reselling the items, because you don't have to spend hours searching for items ongoing. Simply tell eBay what you want on a regular basis, then sit back and let the eBay system do the work!

18

If you're buying items from eBay, why not save and recycle the bubble wrap and postage bags if they're in good condition? Not only are you helping the environment, you can also use them when you start selling!

19

eBay is the world's largest online retailer and you'd be surprised at what you can find, with discounts of up to 70% off the recommended retail prices. One of our staff members has actually renovated her entire home, from the kitchen to the bathroom to the bedrooms, with building supplies and home wares they bought on eBay, because it really does have everything for everyone!

20

Remember that there are thousands of new items listed every day so, before you place a bid, work out what your maximum price will be and stick to it! If the bidding goes above your maximum, don't get caught up in the excitement and go crazy, chances are you'll find another one down the track!

"Faith is taking the first step even when you don't see the whole staircase.."

Martin Luther King Jr.

"If we had no winter, the spring would not be so pleasant; if we did not sometimes have a taste of adversity, prosperity would not be welcome."

Anne Dudley Bradstreet.

21

21.   It's also vital to thoroughly read the seller's terms and conditions before you place a bid. How long will you have to pay for the item, do you agree with their terms and conditions, is their postage reasonable? If you don't agree to any of their terms, it's simple...don't bid!

22

22.　Ask the seller any questions you can think of before bidding, because you are entering into a contract and need to pay for the item. If you don't follow through and pay, eBay can issue you a 'non paying strike' and if you get too many strikes, they have the right to suspend or permanently cancel your account.

23

'My eBay' watch list allows you to keep a record of the seller's responses and answers next to the item. Simply tick the box next to the item you want to add a note to and then click the 'Add Note' box.

24

If you're in the market for new items, you should also check out 'The Big Deal' on eBay **(http://deals.ebay.com.au/).** Here you'll find items that are all new, all have free postage and are all cheaper than the usual recommended retail price. You can also sign up for daily email alerts.

25

Remember that sellers use different keywords when they list their items so, to find the real bargains, try searching for an item with words you may not normally search with. For example, if you were after a pair of 'swimmers', why not search bikinis, togs or bathers instead?

26

Have you ever seen a seller selling an item for 99 cents with a ridiculous postage price? Whilst they may be saving a few cents on the eBay fees, they're not actually doing themselves any favours because they will show up at the bottom of the search results. Why not email them and ask them to use a 'pre-paid satchel' for the postage, to keep costs down? You never know what they'll say until you ask and you can get some great deals this way.

27

Some sellers mention they prefer bank deposit, however don't feel forced into paying via bank transfer. PayPal is compulsory for all sellers and with up to $20,000 buyer protection, it's the safest way to pay on eBay.

28

Always ask the seller for more postage options if they only offer regular mail. Especially if you're investing in a high ticket item, ask them to send it via registered mail and, at $3 for up to $100 worth of insurance, you can have peace of mind.

29

Or how about express post? Like registered mail, you will receive a tracking number, however, in the unlikely event it does go missing, there's no insurance. The great thing with express post is that it's overnight delivery to most areas (check with Australia Post for more info: **www.auspost.com.au**).

30

Whilst the postage can often be too high to buy bargains from other eBay platforms, you don't need to be afraid of buying items from other countries. Sites such as **www.babblefish.com** can easily translate any messages if your seller doesn't speak fluent English or your preferred language.

"The mind cannot differentiate between perception and reality. Dream big, plan big and live everyday as if it were your last. Do what you love and love what you do...."

Amanda Clarkson

"All we see of someone at any moment is a snapshot of their life, there in riches or poverty, in joy or despair. Snapshots don't show the million decisions that led to that moment."

Richard Bach

31

Once you become addicted to buying on eBay (and you will) you can also save sellers to your 'favourites'. This means, every time your favourite seller lists new items, eBay will send you an email so you can check out what they've got available.

32

Have you ever thought about buying furniture, whitegoods or bulky items off eBay, but weren't sure about how to get them delivered? A great idea is to do a search in the yellow pages for local delivery companies or a 'man with a van' who will pick up your item and deliver straight to your home for a minimal charge. The only downside here is that you can't view the item before paying.

33

When you buy an item on eBay, you have the chance to not only leave positive, neutral or negative feedback, you're able to 'rate' the seller on certain aspects of the sale, including item as described, communication, the postage time and postage and handling charges. When leaving the feedback rating be fair to the seller and, if you're not completely happy with their service, then tell them!

34

Give sellers an opportunity to rectify their mistake and remember that one day you'll probably be a seller yourself and expect the same courtesy. Some things are out of the seller's control, such as delivery delays caused by natural disasters, excessive courier charges (which can't be avoided if shipping large items) and postage and packaging costs.

35

If the seller is being unreasonable and you can't amicably resolve the situation, it may be time to notify eBay or PayPal so you can have an outsider view the case and help you resolve it. You can 'resolve a problem' from the won area in My eBay.

36

If you're shopping for a very particular item on eBay and don't want to search through hundreds of items, why not do an 'Advanced Search'? You can search for any item and exclude certain words from the results, search just the titles or the title and description, search for items ending in less than an hour, search the number of bids, location and more!

37

Another great way to narrow your search field is to use the minus symbol to exclude items from your search. For example, let's say you wanted to buy a new pair of leather boots but only wanted 100% genuine leather. You could search for leather boots –artificial.

38

Some sellers don't use the 'Gallery Image' with all listings, so their items end up with a little green camera next to them in the search results. Let's face it, most buyers are too busy to stop and click on every single listing to see a picture of the item, however, a savvy buyer knows that this is where many of the bargains are hiding!

39

Whilst eBay is predominately a place to sell items in new or good pre-loved condition, sellers are also allowed to sell items that have faults or are no longer working (this MUST be mentioned in the description). As a buyer you can take advantage of this and buy these items for parts, if you're handy, and fix them up to resell as refurbished items.

40

If you're handy with a sewing machine, why not buy clothing and accessories that may be less than perfect and repair them? Many sellers don't have the time and let these items go for a steal.

41

Traditionally eBay is an auction site where you bid against other buyers to win. Another great way to purchase items on eBay is to look for the 'Buy It Now' listings. There's no waiting and you can even negotiate the price if the seller is smart and has offered the 'Best Offer' option.

42

When sending a Best Offer, be reasonable with your price because you only have 3 offers available, for each product, in which to negotiate the price. You can also add in extra terms, such as this offer includes free postage to XXXX.

43

If you're interested in buying a product, but don't know what a reasonable price is, you can use the 'Completed Listings' **(http://tinyurl.com/ eBaySearchCompletedListings)** to see what that item has sold for in the past 14 days. Once you know what the seller can expect to receive for their item, you can judge what a fair price to you and the seller is.

44

Another great way to gain bargains on eBay is to search for sellers that sell 'bulk lots' or 'multiple quantities'. You see, many sellers simply don't have the time or desire to list their items individually and are happy to let them all go in one listing. Simply search the word 'bulk' to see how many items are available to be bought in bulk. At the time of writing this book, there were 25,656 bulk items on eBay Australia alone!

45

You may even want to buy a rare or unique item that's not often listed on eBay and, if that's the case, you can tell sellers what you're looking for by using the 'Want It Now' feature **(http://pages. ebay.com.au/wantitnow).**

46

eBay's Deal Finder is a great tool eBay offers buyers. Using the Deal Finder (http://dealfinder.ebay.com.au/dlf/home) you can search for items by price only, such as items under $10, under $25 and so forth…can you start to see why it's so easy to get addicted to shopping on eBay?! ☺

47

When shopping in certain categories, such as motors in Australia or any category in the US, you may see a very low starting price alongside a 'reserve' price. This means the seller is not obligated to sell their item unless the reserve price has been met. This can be frustrating, as you don't know what they are expecting to begin with. One way around this is to email the seller and ask them, straight out, what the minimum price they'd consider would be and negotiate from there.

48

If you are buying high ticket expensive items from eBay always use **PayPal** as they have buyer protection for the customer. This means if you don't get the item you can make a claim back against PayPal and they will recoup the funds for you from the seller.

49

There are also tools such as **www.fatfingers.com** that allow you to find items where the seller has misspelt the vital keywords or brand name in the title. This means that a regular search on eBay won't find this item and quite often there's little to no buyers bidding!

50

The final tip to buying on eBay is to NOT get emotional when shopping! This is meant to be a fun and convenient way to shop and there will always be another chance if you miss out! Quite often sellers will even send you a 'Second Chance Offer' if you missed out on winning an auction and they have more stock available!

50 Magic Tips
for eBay Sellers

1

The number one rule when selling items on eBay is to make sure you use the correct 'keywords' in the title of the listing. If you use incorrect keywords, or spell them incorrectly, then less people will find your auctions, which means less people bidding up the price.

2

When you start selling on eBay, it's important to begin by selling small low-cost items first. You want to learn the ropes on items that are not expensive and that you won't be too disappointed if they sell really cheaply. It's important to build yourself a 'track record' for selling on eBay, so buyers will trust you.

3

Spend more time on the description of your items. We use compelling copy writing techniques and benefit headlines to ensure people get emotional about our items and get that 'Must Have It' attitude.

4

Start off slow and build your credibility. eBay is built on the feedback system so make sure you get as much positive feedback as you can, as quickly as you can. In fact, we recommend getting to 100 Feedback as quickly as you can as it gives your customers more confidence in you as a seller.

5

Create an About Me page as it gives the buyers an opportunity to get to know you more. It's a fact that 17% of bidders look at your About Me page before placing a bid. It also gives you another icon after your User ID, as shown here with the blue and red *me* symbol.

6

When you choose a User ID on eBay, keep it simple so that buyers can remember your name and recommend you to their friends! Don't use numbers or digits like * # @ that are impossible to remember!

7

Don't get fixated on selling high ticket items long-term. We have loads of customers making very good money selling low ticket, low profit items. You just sell more of them!

8

Sell everything you can get your hands on when starting out and, if you can, start you auctions at 99 cents to get more bidders. Open a store as soon as you can, as you'll be able to sell more and save on fees!

9

Poor packaging is a big reason so many sellers get negative feedback, so really take care and make sure the items can't move around during transit. Use good quality packaging…you'll be glad you did!

10

Get to know your Detailed Seller Ratings on your Feedback page. These will affect how your listings appear in the search results.

Detailed Seller Ratings	(last 12 months)	
Criteria	Average rating	Number of ratings
Item as described	★★★★☆	55
Communication	★★★★★	55
Postage time	★★★★★	55
Postage and handling charges	★★★★★	55

"The real source of wealth and capital in this new era is not material things. It is the human mind, the human spirit, the human imagination and our ability to take massive action and our faith in the future."

Darren J Stephens

"Obstacles are those frightful
things you see when you take your eyes
off your goal."

Henry Ford

11

Make sure you offer as many payment methods for your customers as possible. A huge percentage of buyers like to use PayPal, so make sure you have it as an option. Of course, eBay own PayPal and want you to offer this service for ease and peace of mind for your customers.

12

Also, do plenty of research while you're selling off everything and trying to build your feedback score. Look at completed listings in categories you're interested in to get an idea of the price things are selling for.

13

When you finally decide which market you want to sell into, on an ongoing basis, make sure you build a 'cluster' of products around that niche. Whatever you do, don't become a 'junkyard' on eBay. You won't make as much money.

14

Become the expert in your chosen category and do everything to dominate it!

15

Get to know the various icons in the 'My eBay' area. They help you with keeping track of your business and ultimately allow you to offer better customer service.

Icon Legend

Auction Format

Fixed Price Format

Best Offer Format

Classified ad Format

Secon~~~ ~~~ce offer

Checkout complete

Item Paid

Item Shipped

Left Feedback

Feedback Received

Payment was refunded

Item Partially Paid

Request Total

Relisted

16

Keep an eye on your competitors at all times. Sellers come and go on eBay constantly and you'll need to diversify at times to keep the edge.

17

In the early days of our eBay business, we had no less than 50 items up for sale at any one time. This ensured we were earning while we were learning the ropes!

18

Everyone makes mistakes in this business, so have as many listings as possible up in the early stages of your business, because it's best to make the mistakes here rather than when you pick your niche.

19

There's nothing more annoying for buyers than when sellers don't answer questions in a timely manner. Make sure you check your active listings at least 3 times a day to keep on top of this. Remember…if you get slack, buyers will simply find a seller who's onto it!

20

Make sure you constantly test and measure what you're doing so you ensure the best profits possible. Keep updating your knowledge to keep ahead of the competition.

"The past should be a springboard, not a hammock…"

Edmund Burke

"What lies behind us and what lies before us are tiny matters compared to what lies within us."

Ralph Waldo Emerson

21

eBay constantly changes the rules and many sellers don't keep up with them. To be the best at this game make sure you know what's coming up and plan ahead for it. It's change that sees many sellers pack up and leave eBay…we see this as a massive opportunity, and so will you, once you know what you're doing!

22

Never ever sell counterfeit products on eBay. You're likely to get shut down and, if you're a repeat offender, you'll get shut down for good. You'd be surprised at how many silly sellers do this and think they can get away with it!

23

You may not always agree with how eBay set the rules, however, you can make an extraordinary living from the eBay platform if you only abide by the rules. Remember...with every rule change comes massive opportunity.

24

From our experience, deciding what to sell in the early days can take time and lots of patience. Initially we researched for six solid weeks before we found the niche market that was right for us. Too many people give up after a day or two and then say there's no money to be made on eBay. Baloney…there's plenty for those who follow the proven steps and understand that selling on eBay is a real business that takes time and dedication.

25

There's a ton of places you can go to find products to sell on eBay; flea markets, trade shows, garage sales, Craigslist, eBay, government auctions, local manufacturers, local wholesalers, your own information products, importing from overseas, wholesalers from overseas, drop shippers, opportunity shops, friends and family, retail outlets and the list goes on. Get your 'eBay goggles' on and you'll see opportunity everywhere!

26

If you already have a website selling products, why not use the domain name as your eBay User ID? As you grow your business, you can direct traffic to your website and also direct traffic back to your eBay business!

27

It's a good idea to sell things you have an interest in, although it's not vital. At the end of the day, we have a belief in supplying people with what they want to buy and we don't become too attached to the product. Of course, you need to know a bit about your products, as you'll get loads of questions you'll need to answer!

28

Lots of new sellers like the idea of having a drop shipping business. While this sounds very appealing, it's not our favourite way to operate because you can lose too much control. This can lead to a higher amount of negative feedback if you're not on top of things. You have no control over the suppliers when it comes to stock levels and shipping. Having said this, we know quite a few people who do this locally and overseas and say it's a great way to start out.

29

Once you become a skilled eBay seller and have the right education, you can really take advantage of sellers who don't know what they're doing and are simply copying everyone else (who, in a lot of cases, don't know what they're doing either!). You can snipe some amazing bargains from these unsuspecting sellers and turn them into big juicy profits. In fact, one of our staff members does this regularly and makes huge profits from the mistakes of other sellers. Oh well, as they say, all is fair in love and war ;-)

30

Did you know you can sell your services on eBay? If you're a landscaper, gardener, masseuse, home decorator, graphic designer, printer, etc, there's an area on eBay called 'Classifieds' where you can promote your business. This is great if you don't want to hold stock and already have an existing business. Not only that, it's a great way to get more streams of income!

"Success is a journey through your whole life, not a single destination. It is a series of right choices…"

Anonymous

"The road of 'average' is paved by good intentions; the road of 'greatness' is paved with accomplishments…"

Anonymous

31

Another great way to research 'what's hot and what's not' on eBay is through a third party search tool called Terapeak. We've been using this research tool for years now and honestly couldn't run our eBay business without it. You can see who's making money, who's not and where buyers are spending up big! This tool will give you so many hot ideas, we could go on for chapters here just talking about the benefits. To find out more about this hot research tool go to:

http://tinyurl.com/BiddingBuzzTerapeak

32

Visit 'eBay Pulse' to find the most popular searches and the largest stores, as well as the most watched items. There's a drop down menu where you can search all the different categories you're interested in. A fantastic way for you to get ideas on things you could sell.

33

As you grow your business, it's going to get harder and harder to stay on top of the many daily tasks. Automation is the key to eBay success, as it sets you free, and eBay offers a number of tools to help you with this.

34

Once you start to automate your business, you then have time to think about how you're going to grow it. On the other hand, once you automate a lot of the daily tasks, you may want to enjoy some time out with friends and family and simply enjoy the amazing lifestyle you've created.

35

Communication is one of the biggest success keys for selling on eBay. Make sure you let your customer know what's happening at all times so they don't get anxious.

36

Did you know you cannot leave buyers a negative or neutral feedback? eBay wants to ensure the buyer has the best shopping experience, so that they come back for more! We recommend setting up the system so that you leave positive feedback for your customer as soon they pay for the item. It helps to foster a positive relationship from the very beginning.

37

As a seller, no matter how hard you try to please every buyer, there will be times when you get negative feedback. In this instance why not contact the buyer and see if you can do anything to get them to remove it. We've done this on a few occasions and had a positive outcome achieved.

38

Make sure you know what you can and cannot sell on eBay before you start. There are strict rules and guidelines, so beware. If you visit the eBay 'site map' you'll see it under Rules and Policies.

39

Whatever you do, never be a 'non-performing' seller. By this we mean someone who makes a sale with no intention of sending the item. If you list an item and sell it, it's considered a contract between two parties that must be followed through.

40

Always be aware of your language when writing up your item descriptions. Many sellers don't think about how they're coming across and appear rude and untrusting of the buyer. This may sound obvious but you'd be amazed at how many sellers we come across like this!

"In order for you to succeed, you must continually point your life in the direction of your desired destination."

Anonymous

"There is no man who continues on the journey of success who refuses to take responsibility for his actions."

Anonymous

41

Never include spam words in your title description or you'll be pulled down and given a warning, if not worse! An example would be 'similar to Christian Dior'. What you're doing here is targeting traffic that's interested in Christian Dior products and it's not permitted on eBay.

42

Do you know what 'shill bidding' is? It's when you get friends, family, work mates or people you know to bid on your auctions. It's against eBay policies and if caught you'll likely get suspended indefinitely and even fined. It's not worth it, so don't go there and once you're selling hot, in demand products you won't need to!

43

Did you know around 70,000 new members join eBay daily?
This means new opportunity comes along each and every day. Never buy into the misconception that eBay is full and there's no money to be made ;-)

44

Never ship a parcel to a winning buyer until payment has cleared. We've heard many a story where sellers have lost out this way. Also, if the buyer chooses to put the money into your bank account, wait until it clears before you ship.

45

The best way to avoid unhappy eBay experiences is to have clear, open communication with buyers and bidders at all times. This is a real business so treat it with the respect and seriousness it deserves. You'll be glad you did when it starts to give you the lifestyle you've always wanted!

46

Make sure you only ship items to the same address that's verified and confirmed through PayPal. The last thing you want is for parcels to go missing!

47

A big 'no no' as a seller is to sell your items outside of eBay. Often buyers will contact you and ask you to close the auction early for a quick sale. Always decline politely. This is majorly against eBay rules because they have spent a lot of time, money and effort bringing the buyers to the site and, the truth is, the fees you pay for this scale of marketing and advertising are really reasonable!

48

Always have lots of clear photos in your listings so buyers can clearly see what they are getting. Even if there are damages or scratches, etc, make them visible to the buyer to avoid negative feedback.

49

Even though you can no longer sell digital
books on eBay, you can certainly sell CD's and
DVD's, so why not put the information to disc?
A CD or DVD has a higher perceived value so
you'll probably make more money as well!

50

Remember...growing a sustainable, long-term and profitable eBay business will take time and effort. Making money on eBay isn't one of those 'get rich overnight' types of businesses so be clear about your outcomes from the start. From our twenty-five plus years in business, never have we seen or experienced a business so fun, flexible and profitable than an eBay business. We would recommend it to anyone who had the desire to make either a part or full time income, from home, using the Internet.

"When wrong perceptions are replaced by winning attitudes, anything can happen…"

Anonymous

"People who say it can't be done shouldn't interrupt those who are doing it…"

Anonymous

Final Thoughts

We hope you've really enjoyed reading this book and have taken some great tips on board to help you grow your own exciting, profitable and automated eBay business.

Starting and growing a business of any sort including eBay, takes self-belief, time, dedication, effort and constant action.

By reading this book, you have taken important steps towards creating your own massive success and now all you need to do is stay focused and clear on your outcome.

Keep Learning and growing

Because we've only scratched the surface of what's possible with having an eBay business, it is paramount that you keep learning and following in the steps of others who have the results you're looking for.

Share your dreams with those who encourage you and have your best interests at heart and if possible avoid the ones that tell you that making a great living on eBay is not possible. Anything is possible if you put your mind and heart into it.

If you would like to find out more about our eBay Magic courses and how we mentor people all over the world, go to the link at the bottom of this page and request your free report and DVD valued at $97. We have a team of mentors and course advisors who can point you in the right direction for you if you want to fast track your success.

Get the Best Mentors

The biggest reasons we have been able to fast track our eBay and business success so quickly is because we surround ourselves with the best mentors we can find. No matter where they are in the world!

Have you heard the saying "Success leaves a trail?" We live by this mantra…and if we could offer you one golden gem of advice this would be to follow in the footsteps of only those who have the results you want as no one else is qualified to give you advice. It will save you years of frustration and costly mistakes and make your journey easier.

Remember…you can always get more money but never more time…

Make It Happen For You Now

Tony Robbins says…"You have two things in life…either a result or a story of why things didn't work out for you"…

Right now is your chance to finally get the life you want by taking action and believing it's possible for you.

Of the hundreds of people we mentor, there is one common question that comes up in nearly every conversation when we're helping people become successful.

The question is… "Is it easy, Does it work and Can I do it?"

The answer to that is simply…"If you believe it is possible, follow proven systems and steps, believe in yourself and take the right action…anything is possible."

It's up to you…

See you on top of our eBay Magic Mountain

Warmly,

Matt & Amanda

"Helping You Become Cash & Time Rich with eBay"

FREE BONUS

To Claim Your
FREE Report, Your
DVD & Special
Audio MP3 Gift
With A Total Value
of **$297** visit...

www.biddingbuzz.com/book

MATT CLARKSON

When Matt Clarkson left school at 16 to become a hands on carpenter the last place you would expect him to end up is running a multinational business specialising in eBay education, but that's exactly what happened.

After initially spending 15 years working in the construction industry on projects ranging from simple homes, mega mansions, high rise commercial buildings and block buster film sets; Matt is now a bestselling author and internati. expert in Internet Marketing and in particular eBay business development.

His previous experience in construction and Project Management of multimillion dollar mining and construction projects, has enabled him to manage and grow Bidding Buzz from a home based business into a multimillion dollar company in only 3 fast paced years.

After realizing that he needed to make changes in his life and wanting to forge into a brand new industry, Matt and his partner Amanda began selling on eBay in early 2006 and quickly established themselves as one of Australia's fastest growing eBay businesses.

They had actually created one of the world's leading eBay business systems, enabling people to establish and automate their eBay business up to 90%. It was only a matter of time before they knew they had to share this system with the world and quickly built Bidding Buzz into a global corporation, with successful and happy customers all over the world.

Now with students in Australia, the United States, the United Kingdom, Ireland, Hong Kong, Indonesia, Sweden, Malaysia and beyond, with a support team of 16 staff members, Matt along with Amanda, is leading the Bidding Buzz phenomenon across the globe. The future is looking bright not only for Bidding Buzz, but for the thousands of people who have now studied their eBay business systems and are making positive changes for themselves and their families.

AMANDA CLARKSON

Amanda is a passionate entrepreneur who left school at age 16 and has had 33 jobs and has gone on to establish and run 11 businesses over the last 20 years.

Amanda's eBay business, which she started with a credit card in Feb 06 was a run away success and is still forging ahead to this day. Now, along with her husband Matt, she shows everyday people how to become cash and time rich with eBay through their simple, and inspiring eBay education courses.

This amazing journey has seen her now present to thousands of people, from all walks of life, ages and backgrounds around the world, including Australia, London and America.

As a result, everyday people are now living the 'eBay lifestyle' enjoying more time and more income for themselves and their families.

Her deep desire to help and inspire people to improve their lives both financially and personally, coupled with the powerful

Bidding Buzz eBay education programs, has driven her to the top of the business and online community around the world.

Amanda's vision is to help as many people as possible live life more on their own terms instead of someone else's through The Magic Of Making Money On eBay.

More Titles Available Now Or Coming To All Good Bookshops.

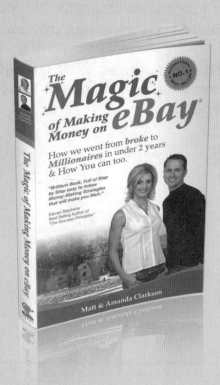

ORDER ON-LINE & SAVE AT

www.BiddingBuzz.com.au

More Titles Available Now Or Coming To All Good Bookshops.

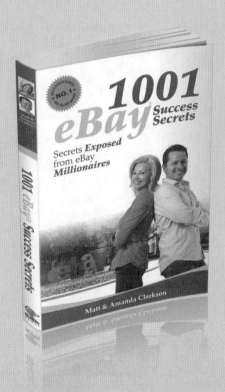

ORDER ON-LINE & SAVE AT

www.BiddingBuzz.com.au